BATS
the
Night
Fliers

BATS
the
Night
Fliers

by Anabel Dean
illustrated by L'Enc Matte

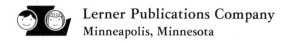

Lerner Publications Company
Minneapolis, Minnesota

Cover photograph by S. C. Bisserot of Bruce Coleman Incorporated

LIBRARY OF CONGRESS CATALOGING IN PUBLICATION DATA

Dean, Anabel.
  Bats: the night fliers.

  SUMMARY: A study of the evolution, physical character-
istics, and living habits of bats, their relationship to man, and
the myths and superstitions surrounding them.

  1. Bats—Juvenile literature. [1. Bats] I. Matte, L'Enc, illus.
II. Title.

QL737.C5D4 1974   559'.4   73-11975
ISBN 0-8225-0291-7

Published simultaneously in Canada by J. M.
Dent & Sons (Canada) Ltd., Don Mills, Ontario

Manufactured in the United States of America

International Standard Book Number: 0-8225-0291-7
Library of Congress Catalog Card Number: 73-11975

3   4   5   6   7   8   9   10   85   84   83   82   81   80   79

Contents

The Hand-Wings

Have you ever seen a bat up close? If you have, you are fortunate. Most people are afraid of bats and draw back in horror at the idea of being close to one. If a bat should fly into a crowded room on a warm summer's evening, some "hero" would probably run for a broom and beat the little monster to death.

Perhaps the reason we are afraid of bats is that we know so little about them. Bats are nocturnal creatures. That is, they are active during the night and they sleep during the day. Thus we rarely have the chance to see them, and we are not familiar with their habits.

7

Let's find out more about this small creature that causes such terror in people who usually like animals. First, some basic facts about bats. Bats, like human beings, are mammals. This means that their young are born alive and are nursed and cared for by the mother. The bat is the only mammal that is able to fly. A few mammals, such as the flying squirrel, are able to glide from tree to tree, but only the bat has true flight.

Bats make up the second largest group of mammals in the animal world, surpassed only by the rodents. They belong to the scientific order *Chiroptera*, a name derived from a Greek word meaning "hand-wing." By looking at the skeleton of a bat, we can tell why it is called a hand-wing. The bones in the wings of the bat can be compared to the bones in the arm and hand of a human. The long, armlike bone gives the bat's wing the strength to fly, and the fingerlike bones on the bat's wing support the skin that covers the wing.

All bats are further divided into two suborders: *Megachiroptera* and *Microchiroptera*. The prefixes of these two words also come from the Greek language. *Mega* means large, and *Micro* means small. Therefore, the Megachiroptera, often called fruit bats, are large bats, and the Microchiroptera, mostly insect-eating bats, are small bats.

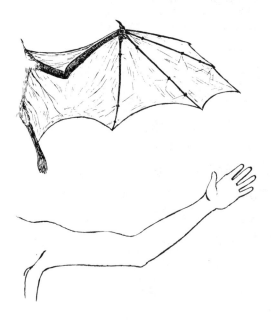

The bones in the wing of a bat are very similar to the bones in a human arm and hand. This drawing shows clearly the thumb and the four finger bones of the bat's "hand-wing."

If you live in the Western Hemisphere, you have probably never seen a Megachiroptera. For some reason, they do not exist in the New World. Perhaps they developed in the Old World after it separated from the New World millions of years ago. The Microchiroptera, on the other hand, are found in both the New World and the Old World. All of the bats in North and South America are Microchiroptera.

The African leaf-nosed bat

The Appearance of Bats

If you examine a bat closely, the first thing that you will probably notice is that the head is held erect, giving the animal an almost human look. Many bats are also distinguished by separate, odd-shaped growths around the nose or lips. These growths, which contain many nerve endings, are believed to help the bats to navigate. They are also one of the reasons why many people think that bats are grotesque in appearance.

The big-eared bat, an insect eater

The eyes and ears of bats differ according to their type. The eyes of most insect-eating bats are very small, sometimes almost hidden from view. The ears of these bats, on the other hand, are very large in proportion to the size of their heads. Insect-eating bats depend upon their hearing rather than their eyesight to help them fly. (In a later chapter, you will learn more about how bats navigate by sound.)

Most fruit bats have very prominent eyes, which they use in navigation. These bats are able to see in the dark, and they are also able to adjust their eyes to bright sunlight. The ears of the fruit bats are more in proportion to the size of their heads than those of insect-eating bats.

The flying fox, a fruit bat

The body of a bat is covered with soft, fine fur that varies in color depending upon the species. The most common color is some shade of brown that blends into the sky at night. During the day, bats often roost

10

in caves. Then, the brown color blends into the darkness of the cave and protects the sleeping bats from
predators.

The bats that hang in trees while sleeping during the
daytime are more colorful because they must blend in
with the different colors of flowers, barks, and leaves.
Some of them look like flowers or fruit as they hang
from a tree. These bats have colors that range from
red-orange to patterns of black and white or even to
all white.

Bats vary greatly in size; some have wingspans of
only six inches, while others have wingspans of over
five feet. But most bats are quite small, about the size
of a mouse. The bones in a bat's skeleton are lighter
than the bones of other mammals the same size. This
lightness serves as an aid in flying. The skeleton of a
bat, however, is heavier than that of a bird of the same
size. This is because the long bones of a bird's skeleton
are hollow, while those of a bat's are solid.

The finger bones in the bat's hand-wing support the
thin skin that stretches from the front legs down to the
back legs. The thumb of the hand-wing is not covered
by this membrane. It is free and is used as an aid in
climbing and holding onto things. In most species of
bats, the wing membrane also covers the tail. But in
some species the tail is left free, and in other species
there is no tail at all.

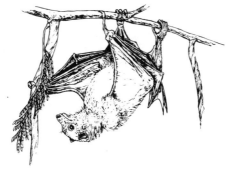

A dog-faced bat grips the branch of a tree with its strong hind feet and the flexible thumb of its wing.

If you have ever seen a bat moving on the ground, you know it is very awkward and appears to "flop along." This is because the hind legs of most bats are too weak to support the weight of the body. However, a bat can grasp an object very tightly with the strong claws on its hind feet, and it will not let go, even when asleep. (Most bats sleep hanging head down while clinging to something with their hind feet.) Bats have even been found dead still hanging in a cave.

The First Bats

We don't really know much about the evolution of bats. No fossil has ever been found of an ancestor of the bat. All the bat fossils that have been found are of bats of the modern type, having wings for true flight. We do know, however, that bats began to fly much later than other flying animals. Insects have been flying for over 300 million years. Birds have been

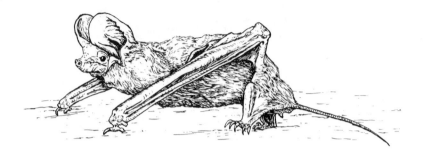

Modern bats, like this free-tailed bat, probably evolved from a shrewlike animal.

flying for about 150 million years. But bats have only been flying for about 60 million years. Therefore, they are still much closer to their nonflying ancestors than are other animals that fly.

Who are the bat's close relatives in the animal world? For a long time, people thought that the bat was related to the mouse. An old-fashioned word for a bat is "flittermouse," and in appearance, the bat does resemble a flying mouse. However, scientific studies have shown that the bat is more closely related to moles and shrews. (The shrew looks a great deal like a mouse, but it has longer teeth and a longer nose.)

The ancestor of the bat was probably a small, shrewlike animal that lived in a tree. While trying to catch insects in the air, this animal probably spread out its limbs and leaped from tree to tree or to the ground. Gradually, loose skin at its sides developed and was spread by the outstretched limbs. This enabled the

*The ancestor of this shrew may have
also been the ancestor of the bat.*

animal to glide from tree to tree much as a flying squirrel does today. As centuries passed, the fingers of its hands, or forefeet, lengthened, and the skin grew between them, forming a wing.

How Bats Fly

In order to fly, an animal must have wings. But the wings of bats are not wings in the usual sense. That is, they were not developed specifically for flight. A bat's wing is made up of a hand and an arm that have been *adapted* for flight.

If you spread out a bat's wing, you can see that the membrane, or skin, covering it looks like the skin between the toes of a duck's foot. This membrane is so thin that the arm and finger bones in the wing can easily be seen and felt.

In order to produce flight, an animal's wings have

15

to be moved by muscles in its body. It takes very strong muscles to push a wing through the air and to keep an animal flying. The strong muscles that move a bird's wings are fastened to a large breastbone. There are two muscles on each side on the bone; one set of muscles raises the wing up, and the other set brings it down.

Bats do not have as large a breastbone as birds do, and they use different muscles to fly. Bats move their wings by using the large muscles in their backs and chests. (Human beings use the same muscles to move their arms.) Some of the muscles pull the wings up, and others bring them down. These muscles are so large that they too can be felt under the bat's skin.

There are other differences between birds and bats that affect their methods of flying. The feathers on a bird streamline its body for flight. A bat's fur is not as well suited for this job as are feathers, but it does help to make the bat's body smooth and thus able to slip through the air.

In flying, a bird uses its tail to brake and to steer. The bat, however, does not seem to use its tail to change the direction of its flight. It uses its wings instead, giving a stronger stroke on one side or partly folding up one wing for a second.

Bats fly through the air with a sort of rowing motion. On the downstroke, the wings come forward and down. On the upstroke, the wings come back and up. The bat

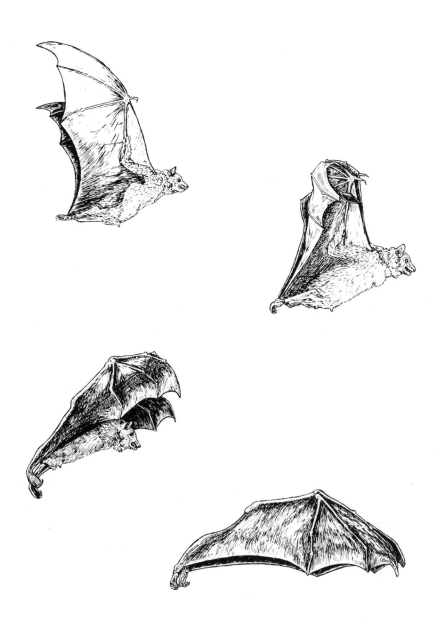

This series of drawings shows the various positions of a bat's wings during flight.

Some kinds of bats have wide wings,
while other bats have narrow wings.

is pushed up on the downstroke, but it goes down a little as the wing is raised. This pattern gives the flight of the bat a slightly wavy motion. But a bat flies so fast that the up-and-down movement can only be seen in a slow-motion picture.

Some bats have narrow wings that enable them to fly and turn very rapidly. Others have wider wings and do not fly as fast. The bats that catch insects for food usually have narrow wings because they must be able to fly rapidly and change directions quickly. Large fruit-eating bats, on the other hand, have big wings, which move at a slower rate.

Bats cannot fly unless their body temperature is at least 80° F. Unlike other mammals, a bat does not have the same body temperature all the time. Unless the bat is very active, its temperature tends to become about the same as the surrounding air. Thus, a bat awakened in cold weather will be unable to fly right away because its body temperature will have dropped too low. It has to move around until its temperature rises to the proper level. Then it can take to the air.

How Bats Navigate

For thousands of years, people believed that bats depended on their keen eyesight when flying at night, just as owls do. One thing, however, always puzzled early scientists. Owls had very large eyes to help them see in the dark. How could bats see at night with their rather small eyes?

In 1794, an Italian scientist, Lazzaro Spallanzani, began experimenting with bats and owls to learn how they could find their way in the dark. He put bats and owls into a room that had been sealed up so that no light could get in. The owls bumped into everything, but the bats were able to navigate in the dark. Spallanzani concluded from these experiments that owls needed some light to navigate while bats were able to fly in total darkness! How did they do this?

To find out, Spallanzani conducted further experiments with the bats. He tried blindfolding them. They flew as well with the blindfolds on as off. Spallanzani thought that perhaps the bats were able to see under the blindfolds, so he surgically removed the eyes from several bats. Then he put these bats and some normal bats into a room with obstacles strung from wall to wall. The bats without eyes could avoid the obstacles and find a place to roost just as well as the bats with eyes.

Later, Spallanzani released the eyeless bats to see if they could find their way back to their home in a nearby bell tower. The next morning, he found the eyeless bats roosting in the tower with the other bats.

Finally, Spallanzani killed several of the eyeless bats and several of the normal bats from the tower. When he opened their stomachs, he found that the bats without eyes had caught as many insects, and as many different kinds of insects, as the bats with eyes.

Spallanzani concluded from these experiments that bats navigated by some sense other than sight. But what could that sense be?

Around this same time, a Swiss zoologist named Charles Jurine began conducting experiments with bats that were very similar to Spallanzani's experiments. He also concluded that bats did not use their eyesight to navigate. But Jurine did not stop there. He went on with further experiments and discovered that bats could not navigate if their ear canals were plugged. Without good hearing, bats ran into everything. Charles Jurine concluded that bats used their hearing to help them navigate. But he did not know how they did this.

Over 100 years later, scientists still did not know how bats could navigate in total darkness. Why? For one thing, no one had really been convinced by the findings of Spallanzani and Jurine. In fact, Jurine's important discovery that bats cannot navigate if their ears are plugged was not ever mentioned in some early 20th-century scientific papers on the bat's navigational system. But perhaps the real reason was that scientists were not yet interested in the theory of navigation by sound. In addition, bats—those strange and unfamiliar creatures—were not considered an important subject for scientific research.

From the turn of the century up to the 1930s, very little attention was paid to what European scientists commonly called "Spallanzani's bat problem." From time to time, a few scientists wondered if the sound that bats made as they flew helped them to navigate. But this theory was never followed up by research, and the matter was forgotten until the late 1930s.

Then, in the winter of 1938, a young Harvard student named Donald R. Griffin began using electronic equipment to record the sounds that bats made as they flew. He discovered that most of the sounds were too high-pitched for the human ear to hear.

Many more experiments followed, and finally scientists discovered the secret of the bat's navigation system. The scientists learned that bats give off high-frequency sounds as they fly. Then they listen for the echoes from these sounds to bounce off of solid objects

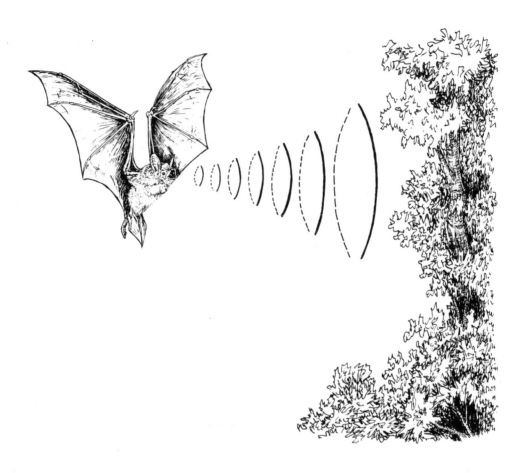

and come back to them. These echoes tell the bats how close they are to objects around them. The tiny bats react at lightning speed as they wheel and dodge, chasing insects and avoiding obstacles.

It was also discovered that bats make their sounds by giving off a series of "clicks." When a bat is flying high in the air where there are no obstacles, it gives off clicks at a slow rate, perhaps only five clicks per second. However, when a bat is hunting insects or is near an obstacle, it gives off clicks at a very rapid rate, as many as 250 clicks per second. As a bat approaches an insect or an obstacle, the number of clicks increases until the sound becomes one loud, continuous scream.

When bats leave a cave or other roosting places in the evening, thousands of them may take to the air at one time. How can each bat sort out its own clicks from the clicks made by the other bats and the noise all of them make as they fly? In trying to find this answer, scientists discovered that even if the bats were bombarded with loud sounds as they flew, it did not interfere with their navigation. Some scientists now believe that each bat gives off a certain pattern of clicks. This pattern enables a bat to pick out the echoes of its own clicks from all the sounds that it hears.

Where Bats Live

Bats are found all over the world. But because most bats fly only at night, we usually do not see them and are not aware of their presence around us.

Looking at the distribution of bats around the world, we can notice two interesting things. First, there are more bats in warmer parts of the world than in colder parts. It is believed bats first developed in tropical regions and have always preferred warmer climates. Second, most species of bats live either in the Eastern

Hemisphere or in the Western Hemisphere, but not in both. The bats in each hemisphere must have been separated while still in an early stage of their development. A few species of bats, however, live in both hemispheres.

The fact that bats fly has contributed to their wide distribution. Bats prefer to stay near their homes, but, like all winged animals, they are sometimes blown away during a storm. If it is too far for them to find their way back, they must make their homes in a new place.

If a group of bats is isolated on an island or at a great distance from other bats, then, over a long period of time, they will develop small differences from the bats they once lived with. These differences will eventually result in a new species. For example, the species of bats found in the Hawaiian Islands are different from the species found in other parts of the world.

No matter where they live, all bats must have a home—a shelter where they can sleep during the day. For millions of years, bats have made their homes in natural hiding places, such as caves, hollow trees, or cracks in rocks. Caves have always been a favorite roosting place. Large groups of bats congregate where the right kinds of caves are available.

BATS MENTIONED OR PICTURED IN THIS BOOK

Scientific Group	Common Name	Location
Order—*Chiroptera*		
Suborder—*Megachiroptera*		
Family—*Pteropodidae*	Flying fox	Old World tropics
	Dog-faced bat	Near East, Africa
	Short-nosed fruit bat	SE Asia
Suborder—*Microchiroptera*		
Family—*Vespertilionidae*	Hoary bat	N. America, Caribbean, Hawaii
	Red bat	N. America, Caribbean, Hawaii
	Silver-haired bat	Northern N. America
	Big brown bat	Africa, Asia, America, Australia
	Little brown bat	Africa, Asia, N. America, Europe
Family—*Phyllostimatidae*	Big-eared bat	Mexico, Central America
	False vampire bat	Tropical America
	Nectar-feeding bat	Central and S. America, SW United States
	Yellow-eared bat	Central America
Family—*Desmodontidae*	Vampire bat	Mexico, Central and S. America
Family—*Noctilionidae*	Fishing bulldog bat	Central and S. America
Family—*Molossidae*	Big free-tailed bat	SW United States, Mexico, Central America
Family—*Hipposideros*	Giant African leaf-nosed bat	West Africa

OLD WORLD

NEW WORLD

Microchiroptera
and
Megachiroptera

Microchiroptera

25

If no caves are available, bats will make their homes in man-made structures. They sometimes use old mine tunnels, culverts, or large pits. Bats are often found roosting in the tunnels of the Egyptian pyramids.

Some species of bats like to roost in houses where people live. They will move into attics, under the shingles and tiles of roofs, and into almost any other place that they can find. Often, bats will make their homes in abandoned houses, where they hang in great numbers from the ceilings and walls.

Bats also make their homes in more unexpected places—for instance, in abandoned birds' nests. In Africa, bats often find shelter in the hanging nests that weaverbirds build in trees. When these birds are not using their nests, some bats find them ideal roosting places.

In the East Indies and southeastern Asia, bats roost inside the hollow joints of bamboo stems. They squeeze

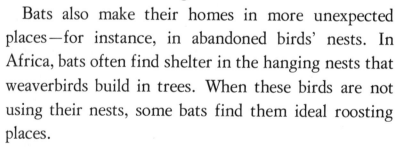

in through a tiny crack in the stalk. These bats cling to the smooth surface inside the bamboo stalk with the tiny sucker pads on their feet.

Some bats in the tropics also use their sucker pads to cling to the slick inside of a rolled-up banana leaf. The leaf unrolls as the banana grows, so these bats must change their home quite often.

The flying foxes, large fruit bats native to the tropical areas of the Old World, like to live in the tops of trees in large groups, or "camps." When they return to their roosting places in the early morning, they gather in such large numbers that their chattering and fighting disturbs anyone who lives nearby. Sometimes the trees are so full of bats that the limbs bend down or break. Flying foxes hang either by one or both hind feet as they sleep, their large wings wrapped around them for warmth. These bats will roost year after year in the same trees.

Only a few types of bats build their own shelters. The yellow-eared bats that live in the Canal Zone in Central America bite a series of holes across the middle of a palm leaf, causing the end of the leaf to bend over and to form a little tent. The bats hang inside this tent during the day. Two species of leaf-nosed bats in South America also make their homes in palm leaves. These palm-leaf tents keep the bats safe from the hot sun and frequent rain showers of the tropics.

The yellow-eared and leaf-nosed bats are the only bats that are known to make their own homes. All other species make use of the shelter that they find.

What Bats Eat

Most bats eat insects. Scientists who have studied bat fossils are almost certain that, at one time, *all* bats ate insects. Over the centuries, however, some bats have acquired a taste for other foods.

Insect-eating bats consume many different kinds of insects—mosquitoes, flies, ants, beetles, moths. They usually catch insects while in flight. Some species of bats use the membrane that grows around their tail as a "fielder's mitt" when catching insects in the air. As they fly, they scoop up the insect in this tail membrane and then grab it with their teeth. Pictures have also been taken of a bat using the end of its wing to scoop

*An insect-eating bat uses the tip of
its wing to catch a moth in flight.*

a flying insect toward its mouth in the same manner. After the insect is caught, the bat flies along quietly, eating its prey. If a bat catches a large insect, such as a large moth or dragonfly, it takes the insect back to its roosting place and eats it there.

Bats do not depend entirely upon flying insects for food. They will take insects that are found resting on the ground or in trees, such as cicadas or crickets. Bats can often locate such insects by the noise they make. The bat listens to find out where the sound is coming from. Then it follows the sound to catch the insects as they sing in the trees or on the ground.

Several families of bats have members that are *carnivores*, or meat eaters. One kind of carnivorous bat, commonly known as the false vampire bat, feeds on many different kinds of meat. These bats have been known to eat frogs, mice, lizards, and even smaller bats. But most false vampire bats seem to prefer birds. During the birds' nesting season, these bats can be seen flying over and around trees looking for nests with baby birds in them. Some false vampire bats prey almost entirely on other bats, and they are commonly known as "cannibal bats."

Three species of bats are known to catch fish for food. These bats usually live in caves near a lake or a stream. The caves always have a very strong fishy odor, and their floors are strewn with fish heads.

Little is known about the way bats catch fish. All

A fishing bat makes a catch.

fish-eating bats are nocturnal and have rarely been observed fishing. But scientists believe that these bats locate the fish by sending out high-frequency sounds, just as other bats do when hunting insects. Sound waves do not penetrate water, so the bats are probably guided by sounds bouncing off fish that jump out of the water. After locating a fish by this means, a bat flies low over the water and spears the fish with its long-clawed feet. Then it scoops the fish up to its mouth and flies back to the cave.

Claw of a fishing bat

There are many bats in the tropical areas of the Old World that eat fruit instead of insects, meat, or fish. These bats belong to the suborder Megachiroptera, and are commonly called the fruit bats. Among their favorite fruits are bananas, figs, peaches, pears, apples, and mangoes. They are especially fond of green coconuts.

In Australia and other countries in the Southern Hemisphere, fruit bats are found in great numbers. At times, they can be pests. They sometimes alight in fruit orchards in such large numbers that they strip the trees of their fruit. These bats, however, prefer to feed on wild fruits and berries.

Three species of bats drink only blood for nourishment. These species are usually known as the "vampire bats." *Desmodus*, the common vampire bat, is found only in tropical America.

The shape of the mouth and the teeth of vampire bats are different from those of other bats. Vampire bats have a split lower lip and two large incisor teeth that are pointed and curved. These teeth are only used to break the skin of the victim.

Vampire bats always attack sleeping victims. They seem to know when an animal is awake, and they will wait quietly for it to fall asleep. The bat lands on a sleeping animal's skin so lightly that it will not awaken. Then, using its folded wing ends as front legs, it creeps

The vampire bat bites its victim with its sharp incisor teeth. Then it sucks blood from the wound by using its tongue as a kind of straw.

onto the animal on all fours. The vampire bat usually bites an animal on an exposed area where there is not much hair. The lips, ears, nose, or neck are favorite spots for attack. The bat is so skillful in using its sharp teeth that the sleeping animal does not feel the cut. The vampire bat then rolls its tongue into the shape of a straw and sucks up the blood. The edges of the tongue are rolled downward so that the blood flows along the underside of the tongue rather than the top.

Because vampire bats do not eat solid food, their stomachs are very small. These bats usually take about one ounce of blood from a victim every night. This does not usually harm a large animal, but it can kill a small one.

The animals most often bitten by vampire bats are horses, cattle, mules, goats, and chickens. The bats also prey on wild birds and small wild animals. At one time, of course, all of the blood taken by vampire bats came from wild animals. It is believed that they still prefer this type of blood if it is available. In many areas, however, there are few wild animals left, and the domesticated animals in pens are easier to attack.

Vampire bats will rarely bite a human being if there are other animals around. If a person *is* bitten, it is often on the face, hands, feet, or other areas that may be exposed during sleep.

As we have seen, different kinds of bats eat many

Migrating bats

different kinds of food. But all bats drink water. Many bats drink while skimming above the surface of a lake or stream. They dart down and dip their lower jaw into the water to take a sip. If a bat makes a mistake and falls into the water, the accident is not serious. Bats are able to swim, using their wings as paddles.

Migration

In 1769, an English naturalist, Gilbert White, suggested that the bat was a migrating animal. From observation, he knew that there were many more bats in the northern part of his country during the summer than during the winter. He also knew that most bats in the northern part of England are insect eaters. In the summer, the insects that they feed on are plentiful, but in the winter, most insects die or go through the cold months in the pupa stage. In order to survive, he

35

reasoned, bats living in the north must either be able to hibernate or migrate.

Other signs that bats migrate have long been noted. For example, it has been reported that bats have landed on ships as far as 500 miles from land. These bats certainly were not looking for food this far from their homes. Another sign of migration is the appearance of large flocks of bats flying in the daytime during spring or fall. Unlike bats darting and wheeling to catch insects, these bats were flying high and at a steady rate, traveling in one direction. Now and then they would glide to rest their wings. It is believed that these bats were migrating.

When scientists started experimenting with bats, they discovered that some species *do* migrate to avoid cold weather. However, bats do not migrate the great distances that birds do. For one thing, bats do not live in the far north or the far south, so they do not have to fly as far to find a temperate climate. Nine hundred miles seems to be about as far as bats travel during a migration.

Three species of bats that live in the northern part of North America are known to migrate. They are the red bat, the hoary bat, and the silver-haired bat. These bats spend the summer in the northern part of the United States or Canada and the winter in the southern part of the United States. They fly down the eastern

Red bat

Hoary bat

Silver-haired bat

North American bats that are known to migrate

Fruit bats often travel from place to place in search of ripe fruit.

coast of the United States, following the same flyways as migrating birds.

Just like birds, bats know exactly when to begin their migration. Most migrating bats leave the northern part of the United States in the month of September, while the days are still warm and the insects are still plentiful.

Bats also take part in migrations that have nothing to do with the weather. In Australia and other places in the Southern Hemisphere, fruit bats migrate in order to be in the places where certain fruits are ripe. Large groups of these bats move from place to place, following the ripe fruit. They always stay in the same places, and they return to these places on almost the same day each year.

In addition to a migrating instinct, bats also possess a *homing instinct*—the ability of an animal to find its way back to a certain place. If a bat is taken from its home, it will fly straight back when it is released. It seems that bats do not depend upon landmarks to help them find their way back home. Bats taken out to sea make their way home just as quickly as bats released over land.

Hibernation

In the northern climates, as we have seen, there is no food for insect-eating bats in the winter. Although some of these bats fly to a warmer place to live during the winter months, others hibernate through the cold weather.

Bats that hibernate during the winter become very fat during the summer. They usually eat enough to almost double their weight. This is necessary so that they can sleep through the cold months without eating.

Sometime during the fall of the year, when the temperature begins to stay below 50° F, hibernating bats look for a place to sleep through the winter. Deep caves are the favorite hibernating place of bats because the temperature in such caves stays constant. (Most bats prefer a cave where the temperature stays at about 42° F.) Many of these deep caves are used only for hibernating and are not used as roosting places in the summer. Sometimes, however, bats will roost near a cave entrance in the summer and then go deep into the cave in the winter to find the right temperature to hibernate. Bats prefer caves for hibernation. But if none are available, they will hibernate in attics, vacant buildings, or almost any other place that they can find.

During hibernation, all the bodily functions of a bat slow down. Its breathing becomes slow and irregular. A wide-awake bat will breathe about 200 times per minute, while a hibernating bat will breathe only about 23 times per minute. At times, a hibernating bat may stop breathing altogether. Experiments with bats in hibernation have shown that they can live for over an hour without getting any oxygen.

When bats start hibernating at the beginning of winter, their sleep is quite deep. But as time passes, they begin to use up their extra body fat and their sleep becomes more restless. They may even wake up from time to time and move to another place. If water is available, they often drink before going back to sleep. This is necessary because during hibernation bats lose moisture through the thin membranes of their wings.

As spring approaches and the weather becomes warmer, the bats become more restless in the cave. By this time they are very thin and hungry. This makes them quarrelsome and noisy when they wake up. Sometimes they will hang near the entrance of the cave, as if testing the temperature outside. When it is warm enough, the hungry bats will leave the cave by the thousands to start feeding on the spring crop of insects.

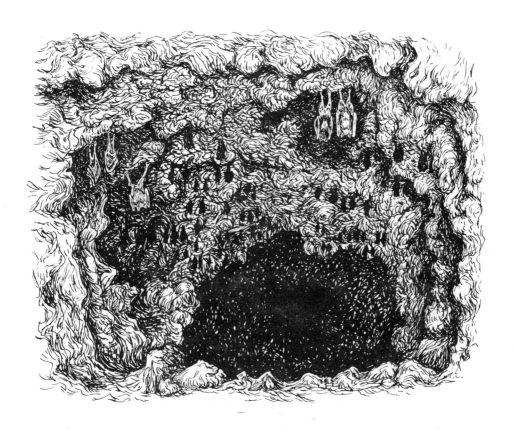

The Young of Bats

Like all mammals, baby bats are born alive and are nourished by their mother's milk. In the spring of the year, the females of some species of bats gather together in a suitable place to have their young. The mother bats will remain in this place, nursing and caring for the babies until they are full-grown. Few, if any, males roost in these nurseries. When the young are grown, the females and their offspring move back with the male bats.

A mother bat nurses her baby.

Most female bats give birth only once a year, and they usually have only one baby at a time. Sometimes, however, twins are born. There are even records of American brown bats having three or even four babies at one time.

Bats are poorly developed when they are born. They are hairless, and their eyes are closed for the first few weeks of life. However, baby bats are born with sharp and well-developed claws. For the first few days after birth, the baby bats cling to their mothers' fur, even when the females are flying. Soon, however, the babies become too heavy to be carried. Then they are left hanging in a cave during the night while the females are out hunting for food. In the morning, the mothers come back to their young and nurse them during the day.

In spite of its sharp claws, a baby bat sometimes falls when clinging to its mother's fur while she is flying. Or an infant bat may fall from the perch in the cave where it has been left hanging during the night. If a baby bat is not killed in the fall, it will probably die anyway. Adult bats fly around and act very upset when a baby bat is on the ground, but they do not land and try to pick it up again. Usually, after flying around for a time, the adult bats will give up and fly off, leaving the baby to die.

Baby bats develop very rapidly. In about a month

they are ready to learn how to fly. At first, they fan their wings to strengthen them while still hanging from their perch. Then the female bats begin to teach their young to fly. They encourage them to try just like mother birds encourage their babies. Very soon, the baby bats are making short, trial flights inside the cave. A little later, the young bats are ready to take their place with the adults, catching insects in the night.

Enemies of Bats

Bats are fortunate because they have few enemies. Most bats sleep in a cave or other protected place during the day. And at night, when they are flying, most other animals are asleep. There are no mammals that take bats as a regular part of their diet. However, such animals as Virginia opposoms, skunks, weasels, and even house cats now and then catch bats and eat them.

A few birds also eat bats. For instance, the screech owl, also called the barn owl, has been known to prey on bats. This is probably because barn owls and bats spend their days in the same kinds of places: barn owls also like to make their homes in unused barns, empty buildings, or caves. The owls probably catch the bats while they are sleeping. An owl cannot outfly a bat, so it could not catch one in flight.

The false vampire bat

Some large snakes catch and eat bats that they find roosting in hollow trees or barns. For instance, the colubrid snake, commonly called the "chicken snake," has been known to eat bats.

As we have seen, large bats are sometimes enemies of smaller bats. The false vampire bat depends on smaller bats as one of its sources of food.

In some parts of the world, bats are a source of food for human beings. In Australia, New Guinea, India, the East Indies, and Africa, large fruit bats are taken for food. They are regarded as an important source of protein to the people in these areas. In Calcutta, India, cages full of fruit bats can be seen in the public markets. They are purchased by the Indians to be used as food. Bat meat is quite dark and tastes something like pork.

How Bats Help People

Many people seem to think that bats are harmful to human beings. This is probably because bats are strange to us, and we know so little about them. The truth is that bats are more useful to human beings than harmful to them.

Bats help people most by eating harmful insects. Every night, bats eat billions of insects around the world. Some of these insects have few other enemies because, like bats, they do not fly during the day when most other animals are out. Moths are one of the main sources of food for bats. Bats help to keep the population of certain harmful moths under control. For example, bats eat the codling moth that attacks apple trees, and the boll-worm moth that attacks cotton plants. In some locations, moths that feed on farm crops make up 90 percent of a bat's diet.

Moths must have been a favorite food of bats for thousands of years. This is evident from the special methods that these insects have developed to escape from bats. When a moth hears a bat flying or giving off clicks, it starts dodging to try to keep the bat from catching it. Sometimes a moth will drop quickly to the ground when it hears a bat and try to crawl under something to hide.

Mosquitoes, which also fly at night, are another source of food to bats. In some areas, bats' consumption of these insects has aided in the control of malaria. Bats

A nectar-feeding bat

also eat some beetles that feed on plants, and harmful
flies that are carriers of diseases.

Bats are also helpful to human beings as pollinators
of wild plants and flowers. Just like the honeybee, some
species of bats feed on the nectar and pollen of flowers.
As bats go from flower to flower, they carry the pollen
along with them. Other bats may pollinate tropical
flowers by pursuing the insects that crawl inside these
flowers to feed on the nectar.

The bat *guano*, or bat dung, that collects on the floors of roosting caves is also useful to human beings. It is a valuable crop fertilizer because it is so rich in nitrogen. There is enough guano in some caves to be mined and sold commercially.

During the American Civil War, bat guano became valuable to the Confederate states as a source of *niter*— a chemical compound needed to make gunpowder. Most of the guano was obtained from the Carlsbad Caverns in New Mexico and from caves in Texas. The supply of bat guano was considered so important to the South that troops were sent to guard the bat caves at all times.

Bats as Pests

Most bats live in harmony with human beings, but some species can become annoying or even harmful pests.

Bats can become annoying pests when they move into a house where people are living. If bats can get into an attic, large groups of them may start living there. Sometimes great numbers of them will make their homes under tiles or loose shingles on roofs. If bats once start living in your house, their noisy chattering and the droppings they leave may become annoying. For many years, people thought that burning sulphur or scattering moth crystals around would get rid of bats. These methods may chase the bats away for a time, but they usually come back. The best way to get rid of bats is to stop up the cracks where they get in. This is often difficult because small bats, the kind found most often in North America, can slip through a crack about one-fourth inch wide.

In certain areas of the world, bats can become pests to crop growers. In the tropics, for example, flying foxes can cause serious problems in some fruit-producing areas. These bats prefer wild fruit, and if there is plenty around, they will not bother cultivated fruit. In some areas, however, so much land is now used for farming that there is not enough wild fruit for the bats. Then they will feed on the cultivated fruit.

The flying foxes usually live in large groups, and they often feed together. Sometimes, a huge flock of them will alight on an orchard and destroy the entire crop in minutes. In order to keep fruit bats from getting started in the United States, the government has passed a law that forbids bringing one of them into the country.

Bats can also harm people by carrying diseases. Any bat can become rabid, but vampire bats are most apt to transmit rabies to other animals. This is because vampire bats are one of the few animals that can recover from a case of rabies. After recovery, they may still carry the disease and pass it on to other animals.

In some areas of the tropics, it is not possible to leave livestock out in the open at night because of the danger of rabies transmitted by vampire bats. If stables are screened or if a light is left burning, the bats will not bother the livestock. However, if one animal is bitten by a rabid vampire bat, the owner usually does not know that his livestock has been exposed to the disease until all of the animals develop rabies.

There are other diseases that can be passed on to animals, including human beings, through the bites of vampire bats. Murrina, a disease that is very harmful to cattle and horses in the tropics, can be contracted from the bite of a vampire bat. Murrina is caused by a blood parasite and is communicated in this way. A vampire bat first bites an animal that has murrina. The disease does not affect the bat at first, and it is able to bite other animals and pass the disease on to them. Murrina is often fatal to livestock, and in time, it kills the vampire bat too.

Strange Beliefs about Bats

When most people think about bats, they think of black, sinister creatures that flit around graveyards at night. People seem to be afraid of bats and to regard them as something unnatural or evil. This fear has led to many strange beliefs about bats. They have been both the subjects and the victims of folklore, myth, and superstition from earliest times up to the present.

In ancient times, bats, or parts of bats, were thought to have magical powers. It was believed that people could see in the dark if they rubbed their faces with bat blood. It was also believed that a bat's head tied to a person's arm would keep him from sleeping.

Bats that were cooked, dried, and powdered were used in medicines to cure many kinds of diseases. Bats cooked in sesame oil would cure sciatica—a disease that affects the nerves in the legs. But if the bats were cooked in the oil of jasmine, they could cure asthma. The body oil from bats was supposed to cure rheumatism. It was thought that bat blood could be smeared on the body to remove unwanted hair. Boiled bat's brains were supposed to be a cure for diseases of the eye, and bat dung mixed with vinegar was considered a good cure for tumors. Hypochondria—an illness in

which a person suffers from imaginary symptoms—
could be cured by a potion made up of bats, adders
(small poisonous snakes), a puppy that had not been
weaned, earthworms, hog's grease, and the thigh bone
of an ox. Of course, if you didn't get all the right
things to go into these medicines, or if they weren't
mixed in just the right way, they could not cure people.

Bats have often been associated with the supernatural. Throughout history, the devil has often been
pictured as a half-human creature with smooth, leathery
wings that look very much like the wings of a bat.
Thus, a bat reminds many people of their image of the
devil. A fruit bat in Australia was once honestly mis-
taken for the devil. In 1770, a member of Captain
James Cook's expedition was exploring this island alone
one day and came upon a large fruit bat. He was ter-
rified, and ran back to the other men crying that he
had seen the devil.

The Maya Indians of Central America had a bat god.
According to their belief, this powerful deity ruled the
Kingdom of Darkness. People who died had to make
their way through his domain to the interior of the
earth. The bat god would bite off the heads of many
of those who tried to go through his kingdom.

The Mayas' bat god was portrayed as a human figure
with the wings of a bat. Archaeologists studying the
ancient Maya civilization have discovered a pit full of

A statue of the bat god, a deity worshipped by the ancient civilizations of Central America

bat bones under the altar of this god. Evidently, the Mayas sacrificed bats to their bat god.

In Finland, some people still believe that, during sleep, the soul frees itself from the body and becomes a bat. This explains why bats only appear at night while most people are sleeping. According to this belief, if you should happen to be out walking at night and a bat flies near you, it is undoubtedly the soul of someone that you know.

There still exists a deep-rooted superstition among many people that bats love to entangle themselves in women's hair. If a bat accidently flies into a room where there are people, its mere presence is usually enough to put all the women into a state of panic and send them scurrying for cover. In a certain part of France, it is believed that if a bat flies into a woman's hair, within a year she can expect a disastrous love affair or, even worse, death. It is interesting to note that there has never been any proof that bats are at all interested in human hair.

Some beliefs about bats have nothing to do with the supernatural. For hundreds of years, the people of Europe believed that bats were fond of ham and bacon. These meats were often hung inside the chimney or in the attic of a house to age before they were eaten. Bites were often found on the meat, and people thought that bats were responsible for them. Then, in the 19th century, two German scientists decided to find out if bats really did like to eat ham and bacon. These meats were placed in a cage full of bats. No other food was given to them. The bats starved to death, never touching the food that was provided for them. The bites that people had noticed on the meat were probably made by rats or mice and blamed on bats that roosted in the attics or under the roofs of houses.

Not all people think of bats as something evil and sinister. Throughout Europe, a superstition about the bat bringing good luck survives to this day. Europeans may nail a dead bat over the door of a house, stable, or barn. This is supposed to bring good luck to the occupants of these dwellings. (In other parts of the world, a horseshoe is sometimes nailed over a door for the same purpose.)

In China and other Eastern countries, the bat has long been considered a symbol of good fortune. Oriental

Bats with outspread wings appear in this design originally used on an embroidered Chinese robe.

people believe that the bat can bring happiness and long life. Chinese greeting cards often have a picture of a bat on them as a token of good wishes from the sender. The figure of a bat has been used in designs on jade and lacquerware and in paintings and prints.

Conclusion

Although often unseen and unnoticed, bats are ancient animals that have lived near people for centuries. Perhaps now that you have read this book, you have a better understanding of these harmless creatures that share our world.

Every animal occupies a certain niche, or place, in the natural world. In that niche, the animal finds the climate that suits it, a place to live, and the kind of food that it likes to eat. Over the centuries, each animal has become adapted to living in its special niche. If too

many different kinds of animals try to occupy the same niche, there is not enough food for all. The species that are the poorly adapted for life there will eventually die out.

The niche that bats occupy is the air at night. If you want to see bats in their natural surroundings, find a place where they roost. Then go there at twilight to see them at their best. They will come streaming out of their cave in a long, shadowy line. Watch how they dart and turn, chasing insects and avoiding obstacles that will be invisible to you in the growing darkness. You can easily see how well adapted they are to their particular niche in life.

When you see bats in their natural surroundings, you will understand why people have been fascinated by this unique animal for centuries.